Welcome To The Massive Motorsports Quiz Book

Lunar Press is a privately-run publishing company which cares greatly about the accuracy of its content.

As many questions in this quiz book are subject to change, please email us at lunarpresspublishers@gmail.com if you notice any inaccuracies to help us keep our questions as up-to-date as possible.

Happy Quizzing!

CONTENTS

ANSWERS

FORMULA 1 TRACKS

1. At which track did the first official Formula 1 race take place?

2. In what year did Japan hold its first Formula 1 race?
a. 1974   b. 1976   c. 1979   d. 1982

3. There was only one season between 1950 and 2000 where Formula 1 didn't race at Monza. Which year was it?
a. 1980   b. 1977   c. 1975   d. 1971

4. Which country held the first-ever night race?

5. At its steepest, what is the degree of the banking of the final corner (Corner 13) at Zandvoort?
a. 15 degrees   b. 16 degrees
c. 17 degrees   d. 18 degrees

6. What is the total track length of the Baku City Circuit?
a. 5.491km   b. 6.003km
c. 6.512km   d. 7.101km

7. At which track did George Russell replace Lewis Hamilton in the Mercedes car in 2020?

8. Which circuit has hosted the most Formula 1 races in history?
a. Monaco   b. Silverstone
c. Spa   d. Monza

9. In what year was the Autódromo do Estoril built?
a. 1972   b. 1976   c. 1978   d. 1981

10. Which track did Silverstone alternate hosting the British GP with between 1962 and 1986?

11. In which country is the Prince George Circuit located?

12. Which track is named after a former driver who won 6 races and sadly lost his life in 1982?

13. At which circuit did Max Verstappen win his first Formula 1 GP?
a. Albert Park Circuit
b. Circuit of the Americas
c. Shanghai International Circuit
d. Circuit de Catalunya

14. What track did Kimi Raikkonen make his Formula 1 debut on in 2001?
a. Albert Park Circuit   b. Circuit de Monaco
c. Silverstone Circuit   d. Al-Ring

15. Niki Lauda survived a near-fatal crash back in 1976, but at which track did the crash occur?

16. How far is it from the starting grid to the first corner at Red Bull Ring, in Austria?
a. 177.13m   b. 216.94m
c. 250.61m   d. 278.94m

17. Based on data collected by the FIA, how many gear changes do drivers make per lap at Spa-Francorchamps?
a. 29   b. 32   c. 36   d. 42

18. How many laps are completed in a Formula 1 race at the Shanghai International Circuit?
a. 56   b. 58   c. 60   d. 62

19. When the Autodromo Hermanos Rodriguez Circuit returned to the F1 calendar in 2015, how many of the 17 corners had alterations since the last F1 race in 1992?
a. 0   b. 6   c. 10   d. 13   e. 17

20. How many corners does the Istanbul Park F1 race have?
a. 14   b. 17   c. 20   d. 23

21. At what track did Aryton Senna claim his first Formula 1 win?

22. What is the name of the circuit that held the first-ever Qatar Grand Prix?

23. In 1967, Jack Brabham beat his teammate Denny Hulme by over 45 seconds to win F1's sole race at what French track?
a. Circuit Dijon-Prenois
b. Circuit de Rouen-Les-Essarts
c. Circuit Le Mans Bugatti
d. Circuit Paul Ricard

24. Which German track has hosted just one F1 race but saw the death of Jean Bahru in one of the support races?

25. In 1960 Ferrari chose not to attend the final race of the season in America at a track more known for Nascar. What is the name of the track?

26. In what year did the only ever Formula 1 race at the Fair Park street circuit in Dallas take place?
a. 1984   b. 1986   c. 1989   d. 1993

27. At which track based near Lisbon did Stirling Moss win the Portuguese Grand Prix in 1959?

28. Lorenzo Bandini claimed his only win in 1964 at what Austrian GP track?
a. Zeltweg Airfield   b. Zeltweg-Südring
c. A1-Ring   d. Österreichring

29. In 2020 the Portimao Circuit hosted its first-ever Formula 1 Grand Prix. Who was the race winner?

30. At what track is the famous Copse Corner?

31. Mike Hawthorn claimed the 1958 Drivers Championship at the Ain-Diab Circuit. In which country would you find this track?

32. The record for the fastest-ever pitstop was broken on Max Verstappens's car in 2019 at just 1.82 seconds. At which track was this new record set?

33. What is the longest track ever to host a Formula 1 race, with one lap being over 16 miles (25.8 km) long?
a. Circuit de la Sarthe
b. Nürburgring Nordschleife
c. Pescara Circuit

34. In what direction do the cars drive at the Marina bay street circuit?
a. Clockwise   b. Anti-clockwise

35. Which American track featured in the first-ever Formula 1 season?

36. Which circuit has hosted more F1 races as of January 2023: Monaco or Silverstone?

37. What year did the Belgian track, Circuit Zolder, first feature on the Formula 1 calendar?
a. 1968   b. 1973   c. 1978   d. 1983

38. Scandinavian Raceway, which hosted Formula 1 races from 1973 to 1978, is based in which country?

39. Which Malaysian track was used to hold Formula 1 races between 1999 and 2017?

40. In what country is the Yas Marina Circuit?
a. Saudi Arabia   b. Oman
c. UAE   d. Qatar

41. How many Formula 1 races were held at Long Beach Street Circuit?
a. 2   b. 5   c. 8   d. 12

42. Autodromo Internacional do Rio de Janeiro hosted ten Formula 1 races. Nine of them were in what decade?

43. The Formula 1 track known as AVUS, based in Berlin, hosted one Formula 1 Grand Prix in 1959. How many corners did it have?
a. 4   b. 6   c. 8   d. 32

44. The Indian Grand Prix was hosted at which circuit between 2011 and 2013?

45. Circuit Bremgarten is based in what Swiss city?
a. Zurich   b. Geneva   c. Basel   d. Bern

46. How many corners does the Circuit de Monaco have?
a. 14   b. 16   c. 18   d. 20

47. In which year did the now-closed Montjuic Circuit in Barcelona host its last-ever Formula 1 Grand Prix?
a. 1972   b. 1973   c. 1974   d. 1975

48. Hosting its first Formula 1 Grand Prix in 2004, how much did the construction of the Shanghai International Circuit cost?
a. $200 Million   b. $300 Million
c. $450 Million   d. $700 Million

49. At 1:35.761, which driver holds the lap record at the now-banned Sochi Autodrom?
a. Lewis Hamilton   b. Charles Leclerc
c. Sebastian Vettel   d. Max Verstappen

50. What Spanish city hosted the Formula 1 European Grand Prix between 2008 and 2012?
a. Madrid   b. Valencia
c. Barcelona   d. Seville

REGULATION CHANGES

1. In what year was the Halo permanently introduced into the design of Formula 1 cars?
a. 2016   b. 2017   c. 2018   d. 2019

2. Between 1950 and 1953, what was the maximum engine size for a Formula 1 car?
a. 1200cc   b. 1500cc   c. 1800cc

3. In what year were crash helmets made compulsory in Formula 1?
a. 1952   b. 1958
c. 1964   d. They always have been

4. In 1961 a minimum weight requirement was introduced for all F1 cars. what was the weight?
a. 400kg   b. 425kg
c. 450kg   d. 475kg

5. 1966 brought a whole host of regulation updates, one of which was making all aerodynamics fixed (or immobile). This resulted in the loss of what type of braking?

6. What former barrier materials were banned after Lorenzo Baldini's fatal crash in 1967?

7. In order to improve safety, what document did the FIA release for the drivers in 2022?

8. In what year were numbers first assigned to drivers?
a. 1954   b. 1962   c. 1973   d. 1979

9. As of 2023, the FIA states that the pit lane must have a minimum length of 80m, but what is the minimum width?
a. 10m   b. 12m   c. 14m   d. 16m

10. From 1982 to 2022, what type of floor was banned from Formula 1 cars?

11. First issued in the 1990s by the FIA, what licence do drivers need in order to drive in Formula 1?

12. In what year were turbocharged engines banned?
a. 1989   b. 1992   c. 1995   d. 1998

13. Between 1982 and 2010, what could be done to the car during the race?

14. An incident involving Rubens Barichello and Michael Schumacher resulted in what rule change mid-way through the 2002 F1 season?

15. What year was qualifying one to three introduced as part of the race weekend?
a. 2000   b. 2002   c. 2004   d. 2006

16. Who has been the sole tyre provider to Formula 1 since 2010?

17. In 1958 the rules on fuel changed so that only what type of fuel could be used?

18. What is the yellow flag used to indicate?

19. Why would a black flag with an orange circle in the middle be waved?

20. If a driver has been disqualified at a race, what colour flag will be waved at them?

21. How many drivers are a team permitted to use per season?
a. 4   b. 5   c. 6   d. 7

22. How many laps of green flag racing must occur for any points to be awarded?
a. 1   b. 2   c. 4   d. 6

23. If a driver is referring to a 'flatspot' what part of the car are they talking about?

24. What does the acronym DRS stand for?

25. In which year were sponsorships first seen in Formula 1?
a. 1966   b. 1968   c. 1970   d. 1972

26. How long is the maximum length that a Grand Prix, without a suspension, can run for?
a. 1 hours 45 minutes
b. 2 hours
c. 2 hours 15 minutes
d. 2 hours 30 minutes

27. HANS devices are required in all Formula cars, but what part of the body are they designed to protect?

28. What is the name given to the car that leads the 'Warm-Up' lap and is deployed when there is danger on track to limit speed?

29. The acronym ERS stands for what?
a. Emergency Radio System
b. Energy Recovery Systems
c. Emergency Race Scores
d. Engine Resilience System

30. Since 2010, how much fuel is required to be in the tank for testing at the end of a race?

31. What does the French phrase 'Parc ferme' translate to in English?

32. Formula 1 Tracks are split up into how many sectors?

33. How long are the practice sessions on a race weekend usually?

34. How many points are awarded for winning a race in 2023?

35. The fastest lap of each race is given one bonus championship point. For what reason may the point not be awarded to the driver that set the fastest lap?

36. How is the championship decided if there is a tie for points?

37. If a pitted car is released into the path of another car in the pit lane, that is considered what?

38. At what race in 2016, were limitations lifted on team-to-driver communications?
a. Hungarian GP   b. German GP
c. Bahrain GP   d. Spanish GP

39. How many FIA super licence points are required to drive in Formula 1 in 2023?
a. 10   b. 25   c. 40   d. 100

40. Each driver gets 12 points on their licence and can have points added for driving offences committed in races. If they reach 12 points, what is the punishment given by the FIA?

41. If a race is dry, how many tyre compounds are all cars required to use during a race?

42. What colour lights are displayed before the start of a race?

43. Between 2014 and 2021, what type of tyres were cars that qualified in the top 10 required to use?
a. Q1   b. Q2   c. Q3

44. What year saw the introduction of the V6 Turbo-Hybrid engines?
a. 2014   b. 2015   c. 2016   d. 2017

45. In which year were the rear wings widened by 20cm and lowered by 15cm to help increase downforce and overall speed?
a. 2014   b. 2015   c. 2016   d. 2017

46. What type of tyre did the FIA introduce in 1998 to reduce the speed of cars?

47. The 2022 season saw the introduction of what-sized wheel rims?
a. 14 Inch   b. 16 Inch   c. 18 Inch

48. In which year were ground effect cars outlawed?
a. 1982   b. 1986   c. 1990   d. 1994

49. The 2004 season saw the introduction of a 10-place grid penalty for replacing what component during a race weekend?
a. Chassis   b. Aerodynamics
c. Braking System   d. Engine

50. In 2007 the FIA brought in a rev-limit, what was it?
a. 15,000rpm   b. 17,000rpm
c. 19,000rpm   d. 21,000rpm

DRIVER HISTORY

1. Which driver was known by the nickname the Iceman?

2. What is the name of the first-ever Formula 1 driver from Thailand to finish on a podium?

3. How many races did Fernando Alonso go between his 97th and 98th podium?
a. 66   b. 77   c. 90   d. 105

4. Which driver had a helmet design featuring Michael Jackson at the 2015 American GP?

5. Who was the first-ever German race winner in Formula 1?

6. Which Red Bull driver was demoted to their junior F1 team, Toro Rosso, in 2019?

7. Which driver completed a double overtake in the pit lane entry at the 2016 Chinese GP?

8. In their one season as a Formula 1 team, which driver won the 2009 World Driver's Championship with Brawn GP?

9. Who won the first-ever Driver's Championship?
a. Juan Mangel Fangio   b. Giuseppe Farina
c. Alberto Ascari   d. Jack Brabham

10. When Michael Schumacher retired from Formula 1 he had the record for the most Driver's World Championship wins. How many does he have?
a. 5   b. 6   c. 7   d. 8

11. Which driver beat both Michael Schumacher and Lewis Hamilton while driving for the same team?

12. Which driver is known for singing 'Smooth Operator' over the radio while in the cockpit?

13. Who won the 2021 Hungarian GP?
a. Lewis Hamilton   b. Max Verstappen
c. Sergio Perez   d. Esteban Ocon

14. Which driver won the 1982 Driver's World Championship, despite only winning one GP over the season?

15. Which Ferrari driver referred to his car as 'a tractor' in 1991?

16. Which driver won the World Driver's Championship with both McLaren & Ferrari in the 1970s and 80s?

17. Which two sons of former World Driver's Champions also won their own World Driver's Championships?

18. Which driver was the first to claim a win in both Indycar and Formula 1?
a. Mario Andretti   b. Jim Clark
c. Denny Hulme   d. Ronnie Peterson

19. Which driver won the World Driver's Championship by a single point in 1976, by finishing 3rd at Suzuka in the final race of the season after his title rival withdrew from the race over safety concerns?
a. Emerson Fittipaldi   b. James Hunt
c. Jody Scheckter   d. Niki Lauda

20. Jackie Stewart won 3 World Driver's Championships, but in what years did he achieve these wins?
a. 1968, 1970 & 1973   b. 1967, 1969 & 1971
c. 1969, 1971 & 1973   d. 1969, 1972 & 1974

21. Who was the first-ever, and currently only, Polish driver to claim a win in Formula 1, doing so in 2008?

22. Who was the first female driver to score a point in Formula 1?

23. Which driver was involved in an accident which saw his vehicle catch on fire at the 2020 Bahrain GP?
a. Daniil Kvyat   b. Daniel Ricciardo
c. Alexander Albon   d. Romain Grosjean

24. Which Japanese driver made his F1 debut at the 2009 Brazilian GP in place of Timo Glock who was injured?

25. Which driver won the 1963 & 1965 Driver's World Championships?
a. Graham Hill   b. Jim Clark
c. Jack Brabham   d. Emerson Fittipaldi

26. Which British driver, who was knighted in 2000, is widely regarded as the best driver ever not to win a World Driver's Championship?

27. How many race entries does Rubens Barichello have?
a. 261   b. 296   c. 326   d. 367

28. Michael Schumacher got his first race as a substitute for a driver who had been imprisoned for aggravated assault. What was the driver's name?

29. Which Australian driver is known for drinking champagne out of his boot after winning a race?

30. What nationality is former Haas driver Nikita Mazepins?
a. Ukrainian   b. Latvian
c. Hungarian   d. Russian

31. Max Verstappen switched mid-season with what Red Bull driver in 2015?

32. What car number was Kimi Raikkonen during his career?
a. 1   b. 5   c. 7   d. 11

33. At what team did Lance Stroll make his Formula 1 debut?
a. Williams   b. Sauber
c. Haas   d. Renault Sport

34. During his career, how many teams did Mark Webber drive for?
a. 3   b. 4   c. 5   d. 6

35. Who was the first Venuzeulan to compete in Formula 1?
a. Ettore Chimeri   b. Pastor Maldonado
c. Johnny Cecotto   d. Onofre Marimón

36. Who was Max Verstappen's teammate when he won his first World Driver's Championship?

37. At what age did German driver Nick Heidfeld make his Formula 1 debut?
a. 20   b. 21   c. 22   d. 23

38. At what team did Mexican driver Esteban Gutierrez start his Formula 1 career?
a. Ferrari   b. Toro Rosso
c. Caterham   d. Sauber

39. After a year-long sabbatical in 1992, which team did Alain Prost join on his return to Formula 1 in 1993?

40. At what age did Mika Hakkinen take part in his last race in Formula 1?
a. 34   b. 36   c. 38   d. 40

41. In what Italian city was Giancarlo Fisichella born?
a. Milan   b. Venice
c. Rome   d. Florence

42. How many races did Jos Verstappen enter in his Formula 1 career?
a. 60   b. 76   c. 90   d. 107

43. What number does Lando Norris race with?
a. 2   b. 4   c. 6   d. 8

44. In what year did Martin Brundle retire from Formula 1?
a. 1990   b. 1992   c. 1994   d. 1996

45. How many cars were impacted when David Coulthard hit the barrier at the very wet 1998 Belgian Grand Prix?
a. 13   b. 14   c. 15   d. 16

46. What was Felipe Massa hit on the helmet by, that knocked him unconscious, in qualifying at the 2009 Hungarian Grand Prix?

47. Brazilian driver Ricardo Rosset entered 33 Grand Prix, but how many did he actually start?
a. 21   b. 24   c. 26   d. 29

48. What is the name of Michael Schumacher's brother who competed in Formula 1 from 1997 to 2007?

49. In his years driving for Mercedes between 2017 and 2021, which is the only year that Valterri Bottas failed to secure a race win?

50. Who is the tallest driver to have competed in Formula 1 since the year 2000?
a. Mark Webber
b. Alexander Rossi
c. Romain Grosjean
d. Justin Wilson

F1 TEAM HISTORY

1. The constructor Alex von Falkenhausen Motorenbau competed in which two seasons?
a. 1950-51   b. 1952-53
c. 1954-55   d. 1956-57

2. How many races did the Arrows team from the UK enter between 1978 and 2002?
a. 151   b. 275   c. 394   d. 512

3. In which country was the Apollon team licensed?
a. Germany   b. Austria
c. Luxembourg   d. Switzerland

4. Bugatti famously entered one race as a constructor, but in which season?
a. 1951   b. 1956   c. 1961   d. 1966

5. What team was licensed in Malaysia and competed in Formula 1 between 2012 and 2014?

6. Michael Schumacher won two Driver's World Championships with Benetton, but how many Constructor's World Championships did the team win during this period?

7. Which British Constructor, that competed in Formula 1 between 1954 and 1960, won the 1958 Constructor's World Championship?
a. Vanwall   b. Cooper   c. BRM

8. In what season did Hong Kong licensed Theodore make their Formula 1 debut?
a. 1977   b. 1981   c. 1983   d. 1888

9. At what Grand Prix did Eagle (All American Racers) get their only win in Formula 1 in 1967?
a. French Grand Prix
b. Italian Grand Prix
c. Belgian Grand Prix
d. Monaco Grand Prix

10. How many of the 120 races that Fittipaldi Automotive entered did they start?
a. 72   b. 84   c. 91   d. 103

11. Spanish team HRT competed in Formula 1 for three seasons from 2010 to 2012. What does HRT stand for?

12. Force India started competing in Formula 1 in 2008 after what team were bought out and renamed?

13. How many points did the British team Ensign score from 1973 to 1982?
a. 0   b. 4   c. 19   d. 43

14. What nation was Jordan licensed to?

15. How many seasons of Formula 1 did Minardi compete in and fail to achieve a race victory?
a. 10   b. 13   c. 17   d. 21

16. Which Italian car brand competed as a constructor in Formula 1 from 1950 to 1960, but never has again?

17. What were Brawn GP renamed to in 2010 after a 75.1% stake was purchased in November 2009?

18. How many Driver's World Championships have constructors Brabham won?
a. 3   b. 4   c. 5   d. 6

19. Which Formula 1 constructor has the most races entered?
a. McLaren   b. Ferrari
c. Lotus   d. McLaren

20. In which year did Haas enter Formula 1 as a constructor?
a. 2013   b. 2014   c. 2015   d. 2016

21. What were Alpine called prior to 2021?

22. Despite zero experience in this role, what team appointed Christian Horner to be their team principal when they started racing in 2005?

23. British American Racing competed in Formula 1 from 1999 to 2005. How many podiums did they achieve in that time?
a. 7   b. 15   c. 25   d. 37

24. Connaught were a constructor in Formula 1 from 1952 to 1959. How many Grand Prix did they enter?
a. 18   b. 32   c. 45   d. 51

25. In which country were the F1 team Fondmetal licensed?
a. USA   b. Sweden   c. Spain   d. Italy

26. When did Honda first enter a Grand Prix?
a. 1960   b. 1964   c. 1968   d. 1972

27. HWM were a British Formula 1 team from 1951 to 1955. What did HWM stand for?
a. Hersey & Williams Motors
b. Hersham & Walton Motors
c. Hall & White Motors

28. How many World Driver's Championships have McLaren drivers won in total?
a. 10   b. 12   c. 14   d. 16

29. In their 5 seasons as a Formula 1 team, how many points did Jaguar achieve?
a. 30   b. 38   c. 49   d. 64

30. In what year did Lotus first become a constructor in Formula 1?
a. 1958   b. 1963   c. 1967   d. 1971

31. Toro Rosso was the previous name for which current Formula 1 team?

32. Which driver achieved Toro Rosso's only win in Formula 1 at the 2008 Italian GP?

33. Zakspeed were a Formula 1 team between 1985 and 1989. Which country were they licensed to?
a. Germany   b. France
c. Belgium   d. Russia

34. In what year did Sauber start competing in Formula 1?
a. 1990   b. 1993   c. 1997   d. 2000

35. In what season did Sauber/BMW Sauber achieve their highest finish in the Constructor's Championship?
a. 2005   b. 2007   c. 2009   d. 2011

36. Racing Point Formula 1 team, who had a short spell in the sport from 2019 to 2020, claimed one win in this period through Sergio Perez. Which race was this?
a. Mexican GP   b. Singapore GP
c. Russian GP   d. Sakhir GP

37. Marussia Formula 1 team competed in the sport between 2012 and 2015. What make of engine did they use in their first two years in Formula 1?
a. Ferrari   b. Mercedes   c. Cosworth

38. What is the name of the team principal of Ferrari between 1993 and 2007?
a. Jean Todt   b. Stefano Domenicali
c. Sante Ghedini

39. Other than Ferrari themselves, which is the only other team to win a race using a Ferrari engine?

40. Cooper Car Company raced in Formula 1 in 1950 and again between 1953 and 1968. How many Driver's Championships did they win in this time?
a. 0   b. 1   c. 2   d. 3

41. Between which of the following years were Dallara a constructor in Formula 1?
a. 1983-88   b. 1988-93   c. 1993-98

42. Which former World Champion driver entered his own team into Formula 1 between 1997 and 2001?

43. Competing in Formula 1 between 2006 and 2008, where was the Super Aguri F1 team licensed?
a. South Korea   b. China
c. Thailand   d. Japan

44. Which team was Giuseppe Farina driving for when he won the first F1 Driver's Championship?
a. Alfa Romeo   b. Ferrari   c. Maserati

45. How many Constructor's Championships have Brabham Formula 1 team won?
a. 0   b. 1   c. 2   d. 3

46. Up until 2021, how many different drivers have won World Driver's Championships with Williams?
a. 4 b. 5 c. 6 d. 7

47. What is the name of the founder of McLaren?

48. At which Grand Prix did McLaren make their debut as a Formula 1 team?
a. Monaco GP   b. British GP
c. Argentinian GP   d. Singapore GP

49. The 2009 Chinese GP saw which current Formula 1 team take their first-ever race victory?

50. How many different constructors have raced at least once in Formula 1 history?
a. 95   b. 126   c. 154   d. 171

ONE TIME WINNERS

1. How many cars were classified as finishing the 1996 Monaco Gran Prix when Oliver Panis claimed his only Formula 1 victory?
a. 3   b. 4   c. 5   d. 6

2. Carlos Pace won his only Formula 1 Grand Prix at his home race, which is in which country?

3. Pastor Maldonado won the 2012 Spanish Grand Prix from pole position. He qualified in 2nd but started pole after which driver was sent to the back of the grid for breaking fuel regulations?

4. After Senna and Prost collided at the 1989 Japanese Grand Prix, which driver won the race due to Senna's disqualification?

5. Vittorio Brambilla's only win came after completing how many of the 54 scheduled laps at Osterreichring, due to terrible weather conditions?
a. 23   b. 29   c. 35   d. 41

6. Giancarlo Baghetti won on his Formula 1 debut, but in what year was this?
a. 1961   b. 1964   c. 1967   d. 1970

7. Jean Alesi was running 2nd in the 1995 Canadian Grand Prix before which driver, who was leading the race, developed gearbox problems that allowed Alesi to take his only ever win?

8. Innes Ireland won the 1961 USA Grand Prix. It was also the first win for his team, but which team was it?

9. Which of the following drivers won the Mexican Grand Prix in 1965, which was the only win of his career?
a. Ritchie Ginther   b. Lorenzo Bandini
c. John Surtees   d. Jo Siffert

10. At which Grand Prix did Robert Kubica claim his only Formula 1 victory?
a. Brazilian GP   b. Australian GP
c. Canadian GP   d. Monaco GP

11. Luigi Fagioli was what age when he won his only ever Formula 1 Grand Prix in 1951?
a. 42   b. 47   c. 50   d. 53

12. At which circuit did Gunnar Nilsson win his only F1 Grand Prix?
a. Monaco   b. Monza
c. Silverstone d. Zolder

13. Lewis Hamilton's teammate at McLaren in the 2008 season claimed his only F1 victory in that year, but who was he?

14. This driver was an 11-time national champion in motorcycling but switched to Formula 1 and won his only race at Monaco in 1972. What is his name?

15. At which Spanish circuit did Jochen Mass win his only Formula 1 Grand Prix in 1975?
a. Circuito de Jerez
b. Valencia Street Circuit
c. Montjuic Circuit

16. Which French driver took his only win at Watkins Glen in 1971 before sadly crashing to his death at the same track 2 years later?

17. Lorenzo Bandini's only Formula 1 Grand Prix win came at the first race at which Austrian track in 1964?
a. Redbull Ring   b. Zeltweg Airfield
c. A1-Ring

18. Ludovico Scarfiotti claimed victory at Monza in 1966, but who was he driving for?
a. Brabham   b. Lotus
c. Cooper   d. Ferrari

19. Jo Bonnier won only 1 race across his 15-year career. How many starts did he have?
a. 104   b. 136   c. 178   d. 201

20. Luigi Musso won his only Grand Prix thanks to a shared drive with what legendary driver at the 1956 Argentina Grand Prix?

POLE SITTERS

1. Up until the end of the 2021 season, how many different drivers have sat on pole position at a Formula 1 Grand Prix?
a. 103   b. 117   c. 125   d. 132

2. Who was the first ever pole sitter at the 1950 British Grand Prix?
a. Reg Parnell   b. Luigi Fagioli
c. Nino Farina

3. Jacques Villeneuve is just one of 5 drivers who scored a pole position on their F1 debut. Which year did he do this?
a. 1994   b. 1995   c. 1996   d. 1997

4. Aryton Senna has the record for most consecutive pole positions. Over which two seasons did he achieve this?
a. 1984-85   b. 1986-87
c. 1988-89   d. 1990-91

5. Which driver has the most pole positions without a race win?
a. Nico Hulkenburg   b. Chris Amon
c. Eugenio Castellotti

6. Of the 68 pole positions Michael Schumacher took, how many did he convert into race wins?
a. 40   b. 45   c. 50   d. 55

7. What percentage conversion rate of poles to wins did Jenson Button retire with?
a. 30%   b. 45%   c. 52.5   d. 62.5%

8. How old was Nino Farina when he scored his last pole position?
a. 45   b. 48   c. 52   d. 56

9. Lando Norris scored his first-ever pole position at which 2021 Grand Prix?
a. Emilia Romagna GP   b. French GP
c. Russian GP   d. Spanish GP

10. Sebastian Vettel is the youngest ever polesitter, but just how old was he?
a. 19 years   b. 20years
c. 21 years   d. 22 years

11. What year did Nigel Mansell secure his last pole position, aged 41?
a. 1994   b. 1996   c. 1998   d. 2000

12. Where did Fernando Alonso take his first pole position in 2003?
a. San Marino GP   b. Malaysian GP
c. Japanese GP   d. United States GP

13. How many pole positions did Lewis Hamilton take in his 2016 title-winning season?
a. 9   b. 10   c. 11   d. 12

14. Which driver has the most pole positions after Lewis Hamilton of all British drivers?
a. Damon Hill   b. Jackie Stewart
c. Jim Clark   d. Nigel Mansell

15. How many pole positions did Graham Hill take over his career?
a. 13   b. 19   c. 26   d. 32

16. Charles Leclerc scored how many pole positions in his first season for Ferrari in 2019?
a. 1   b. 3   c. 5   d. 7

17. Alain Prost retired with the joint fifth most pole positions of all drivers, but how many did he get?
a. 26   b. 33   c. 39   d. 45

18. How many teams did Sebastian Vettel score a pole for before retiring?
a. 2   b. 3   c. 4   d. 5

19. How many Grand Prix did Max Verstappen win before securing his first pole position in 2019?
a. 1   b. 3   c. 5   d. 7

20. Pat Flaherty only won one race from pole position, but how many pole positions did he secure in his career?
a. 1   b. 7   c. 11   d. 16

21. Who ended their career with more pole positions between Michael Schumacher and Ayrton Senna?

22. It is no surprise that Ayrton Senna holds the record for the most pole finishes of all Brazilian drivers, but who is in second?
a. Rubens Barrichello   b. Nelson Piquet
c. Emerson Fittipaldi   d. Felipe Massa

23. Which driver has had the most pole finishes of all Belgian drivers?

24. In which year did Mika Hakkinen get 11 poles in a single season?
a. 1997   b. 1998   c. 1999   d. 2000

25. Who finished their career with more poles, Mika Hakkinen or Kimi Raikkonen?

26. Where did Daniel Ricciardo score his first pole position?
a. 2014 Malaysian GP   b. 2017 Spanish GP
c. 2015 British GP   d. 2016 Monaco GP

27. How many pole positions did Felipe Massa score for Ferrari?
a. 12   b. 15   c. 18   d. 21

28. In which season did Michael Schumacher score his most pole positions?
a. 2000   b. 2001   c. 2002   d. 2004

29. Which Canadian achieved pole position at the 2020 Turkish GP at the age of just 22 years and 17 days?

30. Juan Manuel Fangio scored how many poles in F1 before he retired?
a. 21   b. 29   c. 35   d. 42

WORLD CHAMPIONS

1. How many times did Alberto Ascari win the Driver's World Championship?
a. 1   b. 2   c. 3   d. 4

2. How big was Giuseppe Farina's points margin of victory in the 1950 Championship?
a. 2   b. 3   c. 4   d. 5

3. Who won the 1951 Driver's World Championship?

4. What nationality is the winner of the 1951 Driver's World Championship?

5. How many of the 9 races in 1953 did Alberto Ascari win on his way to the title?
a. 5   b. 6   c. 7   d. 8

6. Who was the first American driver to win the Driver's World Championship?

7. Who was the first Australian driver to win the Driver's World Championship?

8. What nationality was 1970 champion Jochen Rindt?

9. Who was the first driver to win ten or more races in a season?
a. Jim Clark   b. Niki Lauda
c. Ayrton Senna   d. Michael Schumacher

10. Which British driver won the 1963 and 1965 Driver's World Championship?

11. John Surtees won just two of how many races to claim the title in 1964?
a. 7 b. 8 c. 9 d. 10

12. Which constructor did John Surtees win his only World Title with?
a. Ferrari b. McLaren c. BRM d. Lotus

13. Which former winner won the Driver's World Championship for the third time in 1966?

14. Who was the first New Zealander to claim the Driver's World Championship in 1967?

15. At which race did Graham Hill claim the 1968 Driver's World Championship?
a. British GP b. Italian GP c. Mexican GP

16. In which year did Jackie Stewart win his first Driver's World Championship?
a. 1966 b. 1967 c. 1968 d. 1969

17. How many points did Emerson Fittipaldi win the 1972 title with?
a. 40   b. 52   c. 61   d. 78

18. Who was the first driver to get over 100 points in a season?
a. Ayrton Senna   b. Michael Schumacher
c. Alain Prost   d. Nigel Mansell

19. Niki Lauda won the first of his three Championships with what winning points margin?
a. 1   b. 2   c. 6.5   d. 19.5

20. How many of Niki Lauda's titles came while at Ferrari?

21. James Hunt won the Driver's World Championship in 1976, but for which constructor?
a. Ferrari   b. McLaren
c. Williams   d. Brabham

22. How many times did James Hunt get the fastest lap in his title-winning season?
a. 2   b. 5   c. 8

23. How many pole positions did Niki Lauda get in his second championship-winning season in 1977?
a. 1   b. 2   c. 3   d. 4

24. Which driver was the second American to win the Driver's World Championship?

25. What nationality is the 1979 Driver's World Championship winner Jody Scheckter?

26. How many Driver's World Championships did Ayrton Senna win over his career?
a. 3   b. 4   c. 5   d. 6

27. What make of engine powered Alan Jones to Driver's World Championship glory with Williams in 1980?
a. Honda   b. Mercedes   c. Ford

28. How many Driver's World Championships did Michael Schumacher win in the 1990s?

29. What nationality is 1982 Driver's World Champion Keke Rosberg?

30. Which driver holds the record for the most race wins in a single season in F1 as of January 2023?

31. Niki Lauda won the 1984 Driver's World Championship by the smallest points margin to date. What was it?

32. 1985 saw the first-ever French winner of the Drivers World Championship. Who was it?

33. In 1987 Nelson Piquet won his last World Championship. With which constructor did he do this?

34. Aryton Senna won his first Driver's World Championship in 1988. How many times did he start on pole in that season?
a. 5   b. 8   c. 10   d. 13

35. In which of his title-winning seasons did Aryton Senna win by the most points?
a. 1988   b. 1990   c. 1991

36. 1992 saw another British driver win the Driver's World Championship. Who was it?

37. How old was Alain Prost when he won the 1993 Driver's World Championship?
a. 29   b. 33   c. 35   d. 38

38. How many points did Michael Schumacher win by when he won his first Driver's World Championship in 1994?
a. 1   b. 10   c. 17   d. 23

39. What make of engine powered Michael Schumacher to his second Driver's World Championship while driving for Benetton?

40. The 1996 Driver's World Champion was the first time the son of a former World Champion achieved the same feat as his father. What was his name?

41. Jacques Villeneuve was the first driver from what nation to claim a Driver's World Championship?

42. 1998 and 1999 saw Mika Hakkinen win his two Driver's World Championships, but of the 32 races combined over his two winning seasons, how many did he win?
a. 10   b. 13   c. 16   d. 19

43. Mika Hakkinen secured his second title at the final race of the season in 1999 at the Japanese GP. Who was his closest title rival that season?
a. David Coulthard   b. Michael Schumacher
c. Eddie Irvine

44. Michael Schumacher returned to Driver's World Championship glory in 2000. How many titles did he win in a row from 2000 onwards?
a. 3   b. 4   c. 5   d. 6

45. How many Driver's World Championships has Lew Hamilton won as of January 2023?
a. 5   b. 6   c. 7   d. 8

46. Kimi Raikkonen won the 2007 Driver's World Championship in a closely fought battle with two other drivers who finished one point behind him. Who were they?

47. The 2008 season saw Lewis Hamilton claim his first Driver's World Championship in only his second season in Formula 1. How many points did he score?
a. 80   b. 87   c. 94   d. 98

48. Which of Sebastian Vettel's four Driver's World Championship-winning seasons did he win by the most points?
a. 2010   b. 2011   c. 2012   d. 2013

49. In 2016 Nico Rosberg claimed his only Driver's World Championship. How many races of the 21 on the calendar did he win?
a. 9   b. 10   c. 11   d. 12

50. What make of engine was used in Max Verstappen's 2021 World Championship-winning car?

DRIVER RECORDS

1. Which driver is this - They competed in Formula 1 between 1950 and 1956, they are French, started 38 races, got 2 podiums and 18 points in their career.
a. Louis Rosier   b. Robert Mazon
c. Aldo Gordini   d. Henri Pescarolo

2. Which driver is this - They competed in Formula 1 between 1956 and 1961, they are British, started 38 races, got 3 poles, 10 podiums, 6 wins and 75 points.
a. Tony Brooks   b. Mike MacDowel
c. Stuart Lewis-Evans

3. Which driver is this - They competed in Formula 1 between 1960 and 1972, they are British, started 111 races, got 8 poles, 24 podiums, 6 wins, 1 World Driver's Championship and 180 points.
a. Jim Clark   b. John Surtees
c. Tony Maggs

4. Which driver is this - They competed in Formula 1 between 1967 and 1979, they are Belgian, started 114 races, got 13 poles, 25 podiums, 8 wins, and 181 points.
a. Johnny Servoz-Gavin
b. Jean-Pierre Beltoise
c. Jacky Ickx

5. Which driver is this - They competed in Formula 1 between 1970 and 1978, they are Swedish, started 123 races, got 14 poles, 26 podiums, 10 wins, and 206 points.
a. Ronnie Peterson   b. Rolf Stommelen
c. Reine Wisell

6. Which driver is this - They competed in Formula 1 between 1970 and 1980, they are Swiss, started 132 races, got 5 poles, 28 podiums, 5 wins, and 209 points.
a. Dieter Quester   b. Clay Regazzoni
c. Helmut Marko

7. Which driver is this - They competed in Formula 1 between 1973 and 1979, they are British, started 92 races, got 14 poles, 23 podiums, 10 wins, and 179 points.
a. John Watson   b. David Purley
c. James Hunt

8. Which driver is this - They competed in Formula 1 in 1972 and between 1974 and 1980, they are French, started 95 races, got 1 pole, 19 podiums, 2 wins, and 139 points.
a. Patrick Depailler   b. François Migault
c. Jean-Pierre Jarier

9. Which driver is this - They competed in Formula 1 between 1979 and 1986, they are Italian, started 108 races, got 3 poles, 9 podiums, 2 wins, and 122 points.
a. Riccardo Patrese   b. Bruno Giacomelli
c. Elio de Angelis

10. Which driver is this - They competed in Formula 1 between 1986 and 1990, they are Italian, started 76 races, 9 podiums, 1 win, and 65 points.
a. Alex Caffi   b. Alessandro Nannini
c. Stefano Modena

11. Which driver is this - They competed in Formula 1 between 1989 and 2001, they are French, started 201 races, 2 poles, 32 podiums, 1 win, and 241 points.
a. Jean Alesi   b. Olivier Grouillard
c. Érik Comas

12. Which driver is this - They competed in Formula 1 between 1992 and 1997, they are Japanese, started 95 races, and got 5 points.
a. Naoki Hattori   b. Ukyo Katayama
c. Toshio Suzuki

13. Which driver is this - They competed in Formula 1 between 1994 and 2000 and again in 2002, they are Finnish, started 109 races, got 2 podiums and 33 points.
a. Mika Häkkinen   b. Jan Magnussen
c. Mika Salo

14. Which driver is this - They competed in Formula 1 between 1993 and 2011, they are Brazilian, started 322 races, 14 poles, 68 podiums, 11 wins and 658 points.
a. Rubens Barrichello
b. Christian Fittipaldi
c. Pedro Diniz

15. Which driver is this - They competed in Formula 1 between 1997 and 2007, they are German, started 180 races, 6 poles, 27 podiums, 6 wins and 329 points.
a. Nick Heideld   b. Ralf Schumacher
c. Heinz-Harald Frentzen

16. Which driver is this - They competed in Formula 1 between 2012 and 2014, they are French, started 58 races, and got 51 points.
a. Jean-Éric Vergne   b. Charles Pic
c. Sébastien Buemi

17. Which driver is this - They competed in Formula 1 between 2016 and 2017, they are British, started 35 races, and got 9 points.
a. Max Chilton   b. Will Stevens
c. Jolyon Palmer

18. Which driver is this - They competed in Formula 1 between 2008 and 2009, they are Brazilian, started 28 races, got 1 podium and got 19 points.
a. Nelson Piquet JR   b. Bruno Senna
c. Lucas di Grassi

19. Which driver is this - They competed in Formula 1 between 2004 and 2006 but also in 2010, they are Austrian, started 49 races and got 14 points.
a. Patrick Friesacher   b. Zsolt Baumgartner
c. Christian Klien

20. Which driver is this - They competed in Formula 1 between 2002 and 2013, they are Australian, started 215 races, 13 poles, 42 podiums, 9 wins and 1047.5 points.
a. Timo Glock   b. Narain Karthikeyan
c. Mark Webber

F1 THROUGH THE DECADES

1950s

1. Why do some drivers only have half points from winning races?

2. What American series race counted towards the Formula 1 World Championship in this period?

3. Why was Mike Hawthorn disqualified (although this decision was overturned) at the 1958 Portuguese GP?

4. How many drivers shared the fastest lap point at the 1954 British GP?
a. 3   b. 5   c. 7   d. 9

5. How many non-championship races were there in the first-ever season of Formula 1 in 1950?
a. 12   b. 17   c. 22   d. 27

1960s

1. How many of the first 7 races in 1965 did Jim Clark win to wrap up the Driver's World Championship on the 1st of August?
a. 3   b. 4   c. 5   d. 6

2. What type of car engine won the Championship for the last time in 1960?

3. The Ferrari car in 1961, Tipo 156, had what type of nose design?
a. Shark nose   b. Lion nose
c. Mouse nose   d. Frog nose

4. Which German driver sadly lost their life after a collision with Jim Clark at Monza in 1961?

5. What type of Ford V8 engine won its first race in Formula 1 at Zandvoort in 1967?
a. DFV   b. DLV   c. DRV   d. DSV

1970s

1. What is the name of the two men who designed the Lotus 72, 72D, 56B and 78 which were era-defining technical breakthroughs?

2. Which team brought the first turbocharged engine car to the grid in 1977, the first forced-aspiration unit since 1951?
a. Honda   b. Renault   c. Ferrari   d. Lotus

3. What is the nickname for the Tyrell P34 used in 1976 that had 6 tyres rather than the conventional 4?

4. What oil giant left Formula 1 in the 1970s due to an ongoing oil crisis?
a. Gulf   b. Aramco   c. Shell

5. What brand of tyre made its Formula 1 debut in 1977?

6. How many different teams managed to win a race in the 1970s?
a. 5   b. 9   c. 13   d. 16

7. Mario Andretti won which two legendary American series races before coming to Formula 1 and winning the 1978 Driver's World Championship?

8. How many points were awarded for a win during this decade?
a. 8   b. 9   c. 10   d. 15

9. Which driver won the most races in the 1970s with 17 wins?

10. 1973 saw the safety car introduced to Formula 1. What make of car was the safety car for that season?
a. Porsche   b. Ferrari
c. Aston Martin   d. Mercedes

1980s

1. A battle for control and money between two, now-defunct, representative organisations caused several races in this decade not to count towards the world title. what were the abbreviations of the 2 organisations?

2. How many races into the 1982 season did Carlos Reutemann announce his retirement?
a. 2   b. 4   c. 6   d. 8

3. How many different drivers won a race in the 16-race, 1982 season?
a. 5   b. 7   c. 9   d. 11

4. Who won more Driver's World Championships between Alain Prost and Nelson Piquet in the 1980s?

5. How many races did Aryton Senna win with Lotus in the 1980s?
a. 4   b. 6   c. 8   d. 10

6. Which Williams driver had a tyre blowout which ruled him out of title contention in the 1986 Australian GP?
a. Jacques Laffite   b. Keke Rosberg
c. Carlos Reutemann   d. Nigel Mansell

7. What position did Aryton Senna finish at the 1988 Japanese GP after stalling at the start and dropping to 14th?
a. 1st   b. 2nd   c. 3rd   d. 20th

8. How many of the 16 races did McLaren win in the 1988 season?
a. 13   b. 14   c. 15   d. 16

9. What did Alain Prost do to Ayrton Senna at the 1989 Japanese GP to ensure he won the Driver's World Championship?

10. There was only one year during the 1980s when the Championship was wrapped up two races before the end. Which year was this?
a. 1985   b. 1980   c. 1988   d. 1986

1990s

1. How did Michael Schumacher win the 1998 British GP?

2. At what race did Michael Schumacher, Gilles Villeneuve and Heinz Harold Frentzen set the exact same lap time in the closest F1 qualifying session in history in 1997?
a. Montreal, Canada   b. Imola, Italy
c. Interlagos, Brazil   d. Jerez, Spain

3. Which driver set the fastest lap through the pits at the 1993 Donnington Park GP?

4. At which Grand Prix in 1999 did Rubén's Barichello suffer engine failure that ended his chance of a win at his home race?

5. How many race bans did Michael Schumacher receive in 1994 for ignoring a black flag?
a. 1 race ban   b. 2 race ban
c. 3 race ban   d. 4 race ban

6. At what Grand Prix did Senna shunt Prost off the road to claim the 1990 Driver's World Championship?
a. Portuguese GP   b. Japanese GP
c. San Marino GP   d. Canadian GP

7. What was the name of Michael Schumacher's teammate when he made his Formula 1 debut for Jordan in 1991?

8. How many drivers of the 21 starters at the 1996 Monaco GP survived the opening lap?
a. 13   b. 16   c. 19

9. Why was Michael Schumacher banned from the 1997 Driver's World Championship?

10. Which famous engineer designed Nigel Mansell's 1993 World Championship-winning car?

2000s

1. Who did Michael Schumacher beat by 1.8 seconds in 2000 at Suzuka to claim the title that year, saying that it was the greatest race he had ever driven in?

2. How many of the 85 races between 2000 and 2004 did Michael Schumacher win?
a. 35   b. 39   c. 44   d. 48

3. Ferrari asked Rubéns Barichello to move out of the way of Michael Schumacher so he could win what GP in 2002?
a. Malaysian GP   b. Austrian GP
c. European GP   d. British GP

4. Why did 14 of 20 cars pit after the parade lap at the United States GP in 2005?

5. An injury to which BMW Sauber driver at the Canadian GP in 2007 resulted in Sebastian Vettel making his debut at the next race?

6. Fernando Alonso deliberately impeded what driver in their final pitstop during qualifying at the 2007 Hungarian GP, that saw Alonso given a grid penalty?

7. How much did the FIA fine McLaren over the spy scandal, which saw former Ferrari engineer Nigel Stepney send 780 pages of information to McLaren?
a. $10 Million   b. $50 Million
c. $100 Million   d. $200 million

8. At what race in 2008 did Nelson Piquet JR purposely crash to allow teammate Fernando Alonso to pit under the safety car and win the race?
a. Turkish GP   b. Bahrain GP
c. Chinese GP   d. Singapore GP

9. Who did a young Lewis Hamilton overtake in the final lap of the 2008 Brazilian GP to win his first Driver's World Championship, despite starting the lap 13 seconds behind him?

10. Who was the engine supplier for Brawn GP in 2009?

11. Which team won the Constructor's World Championship in 2005?
a. Ferrari   b. Renault
c. Brawn   d. McLaren

12. At which Grand Prix in 2007 did Lewis Hamilton drive into the gravel trap on the pitlane entrance on the 31st lap after Hamilton found himself with the wrong tyres?
a. Belgian GP   b. Italian GP
c. French GP   d. Chinese GP

13. On what lap did Fernando Alonso crash at the 2007 Japanese GP?
a. 10   b. 28   c. 42   d. 50

14. How many races did McLaren win in the 2007 season?
a. 8   b. 9   c. 10   d. 11

15. How many Brazilian drivers competed in the 2004 Formula 1 season?
a. 2   b. 3   c. 4   d. 5

16. Which Spanish driver made his Formula 1 debut for Toro Rosso in 2009?

17. Which Force India driver claimed their maiden pole at the 2009 Belgium GP?

18. The longest-ever qualifying was in the Brazil GP 2009, but how long did it last?
a. 2 hours 16 minutes
b. 2 hours 29 minutes
c. 2 hours 41 minutes

19. What was the first Grand Prix in 2008?

20. What colours were featured on the Renault livery used in 2005?

2010s

1. Which driver collided with Sebastian Vettel at the 2010 Turkish GP while battling for the lead, which saw Vettel unable to continue in the race?

2. How many of the 77 races from 2010 to 2013 did Sebastian Vettel win?
a. 25   b. 28   c. 31   d. 34

3. What position did Max Verstappen qualify in on his debut for Toro Rosso at Albert Park in 2015?
a. 16th   b. 12th   c. 8th   d. 5th

4. Why did Fernando Alonso miss the first race of the 2015 season?

5. On what lap of the race did Nico Rosberg and Lewis Hamilton collide at the 2016 Spanish GP, putting both cars out of the race?
a. 1st   b. 2nd   c. 9th   d. 45th

6. How many days after winning the Driver's World Championship in 2016 did Nico Rosberg retire from Formula 1?
a. 1 day   b. 5 days   c. 10 days   d. 30 days

7. Which Ferrari driver purposely swerved into Lewis Hamilton at the Azerbaijan GP in 2017, getting a 10-second stop-and-go penalty for his actions?

8. How many drivers were out on lap 1 of the 2017 Singapore GP?
a. 2   b. 3   c. 4   d. 5

9. What did Sebastian Vettel do in parc ferme at the 2019 Canadian GP after finishing 2nd to Lewis Hamilton?

10. What size lead did Fernando Alonso have over Sebastian Vettel going into the final race of the 2010 season, only for Vettel to turn it around and become the champion?
a. 10   b. 15   c. 20   d. 25

11. Which Williams driver's car caught on fire in the pit lane after the 2012 Spanish GP?

12. How many tyre failures occurred at the 2013 British GP?
a. 2   b. 4   c. 6   d. 8

13. On what lap did Sebastian Vettel crash out while leading the 2018 German GP?
a. 29   b. 35   c. 44   d. 52

14. How many different Driver's World Champions were there from 2010-2019?

15. Which driver did Mark Webber go straight into the back of in the 2010 European GP?

16. At which Grand Prix in 2013 did Sebastian Vettel get out of his car in front of the main grandstand and bow to it, just after doing doughnuts?
a. Indian GP   b. United States GP
c. Brazilian GP   d. Hungarian GP

17. Why were Ferrari fined $100,000 after the 2010 German GP?

18. A battle between what two drivers at the 2014 Bahrain GP has become known as the 'Duel in the Desert'?

19. Who won the most Constructor's World Championships in this decade?

20. A crash by which driver at the 2012 Brazilian GP ultimately ended the race where Sebastian Vettel secured his third Driver's World Championship?

ANSWERS

FORMULA 1 TRACKS

1. Silverstone
2. b - 1976
3. a - 1980
4. Singapore
5. d - 18 degrees
6. b - 6.003km
7. Bahrain International Circuit
8. d - Monza
9. a - 1972
10. Brands Hatch
11. South Africa
12. Circuit Gilles Villeneuve
13. d - Circuit de Catalunya
14. a - Albert Park Circuit, Melbourne
15. Nurburgring
16. b - 216.94m
17. d - 42
18. a - 56
19. e - 17
20. a - 14
21. Autódromo do Estoril
22. Losail International Circuit
23. c - Circuit Le Mans Bugatti
24. AVUS
25. Riverside
26. a - 1984

27. Monsanto Park
28. a - Zeltweg Airfield
29. Lewis Hamilton
30. Silverstone
31. Morocco
32. Interlagos
33. c - The Pescara Circuit
34. b - Anti-clockwise
35. Indianapolis Motor Speedway
36. Monaco has hosted 11 more, having 68 Grand Prix so far
37. b - 1973
38. Sweden
39. Sepang International Circuit
40. c - United Arab Emirates
41. c - 8
42. 1980s
43. a - 4
44. Buddh Imternational Circuit
45. d - Bern
46. c - 18
47. d - 1975
48. c - $450 Million
49. a - Lewis Hamilton
50. b - Valencia

REGULATION CHANGES

1. c - 2018
2. b - 1500cc
3. a - 1952
4. c - 450kg
5. Air braking
6. Straw bales and also fuel drums
7. Drivers Code of Conduct
8. c - 1973
9. b - 12m
10. Ground effects
11. FIA Super License
12. a - 1989
13. Refuelling
14. No team orders
15. d - 2006
16. Pirelli
17. Commercial Petrol
18. Hazard on track
19. A driver has a mechanical issue and must return to the pits
20. Black
21. a - 4
22. b - 2 laps
23. Tyres
24. Drag Reduction System
25. b - 1968
26. b - 2 Hours

27. Head and Neck
28. Safety car
29. b - Energy Recovery System
30. 1 Litre
31. Closed Park
32. 3
33. 1 hour
34. 25 Points
35. If they finish outside the top 10
36. Whoever has the most race wins in that season, then if that is tied it is whoever has the most second places and so on...
37. Unsafe release
38. b - The German GP
39. c - 40 points
40. One race ban
41. 2
42. Red lights
43. b - Start the race on their Q2 tyres
44. a - 2014
45. d - 2017
46. Grooved tyres
47. c - 18 inch
48. a - 1982
49. Engine
50. c - 19,000rpm

DRIVER HISTORY

1. Kimi Raikkonen
2. Alex Albon
3. d - 105 Races
4. Lewis Hamilton
5. Wolfgang von Trips
6. Pierre Gasly
7. Sebastian Vettel
8. Jenson Button
9. b - Giuseppe Farina
10. c - 7 World Driver's Championships
11. Nico Rosberg
12. Carlos Sainz. Jr
13. d - Esteban Ocon
14. Keke Rosberg
15. Alain Prost
16. Niki Lauda
17. Nico Rosberg & Damon Hill
18. a - Mario Andretti
19. b - James Hunt
20. c - 1969, 1971 & 1973
21. Robert Kubica
22. Lella Lombardi
23. d - Romain Grosjean
24. Kamui Kobayashi
25. b - Jim Clark
26. Stirling Moss
27. c - 326

28. Bertrand Gachot
29. Daniel Ricciardo
30. d - Russian
31. Daniil Kvyat
32. c - 7
33. a - Williams
34. b - 4, Minardi, Jaguar, Williams and Red Bull
35. a - Ettore Chimeri
36. Sergio Perez
37. c - 22
38. d - Sauber
39. Williams
40. a - 34
41. c - Rome
42. d - 107
43. b - 4
44. d - 1996
45. a - 13
46. Metal spring
47. c - 26
48. Ralf Schumacher
49. 2018
50. d - Justin Wilson at 1.94 metres

F1 TEAM HISTORY

1. b - 1952-53
2. c - 394
3. d - Switzerland
4. b - 1956
5. Caterham
6. One in 1995
7. a - Vanwall
8. a - 1977
9. c - Belgian Grand Prix
10. d - 103
11. Hispania Racing Team
12. Spyker F1
13. c - 19
14. Ireland
15. d - 21
16. Maserati
17. Mercedes
18. b - 4
19. b - Ferrari
20. d - 2016
21. Renault
22. Red Bull
23. b - 15
24. a - 18
25. d - Italy
26. b - 1964

27. b - Hersham and Walton Motors
28. b - 12
29. c - 49
30. a - 1958
31. Alpha Tauri
32. Sebastian Vettel
33. a - Germany
34. b - 1993
35. b - 2007
36. d - Sakhir GP
37. c - Cosworth
38. a - Jean Todt
39. Toro Rosso
40. c - 2
41. b - 1988-93
42. Alain Prost
43. d - Japan
44. a - Alfa Romeo
45. c - 2
46. d - 7
47. Bruce McLaren
48. a - Monaco GP
49. Red Bull
50. d - 171

ONE TIME WINNERS

1. a - 3
2. Brazil
3. Lewis Hamilton
4. Alessandro Nannini
5. b - 29
6. a - 1961
7. Michael Schumacher
8. Team Lotus
9. a - Richie Ginther
10. c - Canadian GP
11. d - 53
12. d - Zolder
13. Heikki Kovalainen
14. Jean-Pierre Beltoise
15. c - Montjuic Circuit
16. Francois Cevert
17. b - Zeltweg Airfield
18. d - Ferrari
19. a - 104
20. Juan Manuel Fangio

Pole Sitters

1. a - 103
2. c - Nino Farina
3. c - 1996
4. c - 1988-1989
5. b - Chris Amon
6. a - 40
7. d - 62.5%
8. b - 48 Years old
9. c - Russian Grand Prix
10. c - 21 years
11. a - 1994
12. b - Malaysian Grand Prix
13. d - 12
14. c - Jim Clark
15. a - 13
16. d - 7
17. b - 33
18. b - 3
19. d - 7
20. a - 1, trick question
21. Michael Schumacher finished with 3 more
22. b - Nelson Piquet
23. Jacky Ickx
24. c - 1999
25. Mika Hakkinen had 8 more
26. d - 2016 Monaco Grand Prix

27. b - 15
28. b - 2001
29. Lance Stroll
30. b - 29

World Champions

1. b - 2
2. b - 3
3. Juan Manuel Fangio
4. Argentinian
5. a - 5
6. Phil Hill
7. Jack Brabham
8. He was a German-born driver who competed under an Austrian licence
9. d - Michael Schumacher
10. Jim Clark
11. d - 10
12. a - Ferrari
13. Jack Brabham
14. Denny Hulme
15. c - Mexican GP
16. d - 1969
17. c - 61
18. d - Nigel Mansell
19. d - 19.5
20. 3
21. b - McLaren
22. a - 2
23. b - 2
24. Mario Andretti
25. South African
26. a - 3

27. c - Ford
28. 2
29. Finnish
30. Max Verstappen
31. 0.5
32. Alain Prost
33. Williams
34. d - 13
35. c - 1991
36. Nigel Mansell
37. d - 38
38. a - 1
39. Renault
40. Damon Hill
41. Canada
42. b - 13
43. c - Eddie Irvine
44. c - 5
45. c - 7
46. Lewis Hamilton & Fernando Alonso
47. d - 98
48. d - 2013
49. a - 9
50. Honda

DRIVER RECORDS

1. a - Louis Rosier
2. a - Tony Brooks
3. b - John Surtees
4. c - Jacky Ickx
5. a - Ronnie Peterson
6. b - Clay Regazzoni
7. c - James Hunt
8. a - Patrick Depailler
9. c - Elio de Angelis
10. b - Alessandro Nannini
11. a - Jean Alesi
12. b - Ukyo Katayama
13. c - Mika Salo
14. a - Rubens Barrichello
15. b - Ralf Schumacher
16. a - Jean-Éric Vergne
17. c - Jolyon Palmer
18. a - Nelson Piquet JR
19. c - Christian Klien
20. c - Mark Webber

F1 THROUGH THE DECADES

1950s

1. Car swapping
2. Indy 500
3. Bump starting his car
4. c - 7
5. c - 22

1960s

1. d - 6
2. Front Engined
3. a - Shark nose
4. Wolfgang von Trips
5. a - DFV

1970s

1. Colin Chapman & Maurice Philippe
2. b - Renault
3. Centipede
4. c - Shell
5. Michelin
6. c - 13
7. Indy 500 & Daytona 500

8. b - 9
9. Niki Lauda
10. a - Porsche

1980s

1. FISA & FOCA
2. a - 2
3. d - 11
4. They both won 3
5. b - 6
6. d - Nigel Mansell
7. b - 2nd
8. c - 15, and in ten of them they finished 1-2
9. Turned into him
10. a - 1985

1990s

1. In the pits
2. d - Jerez, Spain
3. Aryton Senna
4. Brazil GP
5. b - 2 race ban
6. b - Japanese GP, Suzuka
7. Andrea de Cesaris
8. b - 16
9. Trying to cause a collision with Jacques Villeneuve
10. Adrian Newey

2000s

1. Mika Hakkinen
2. d - 48
3. b - Austrian GP
4. Michelin tyre safety
5. Robert Kubica
6. Lewis Hamilton
7. c - $100 Million
8. d - Singapore GP
9. Timo Glock
10. Mercedes
11. b - Renault
12. d - Chinese GP
13. c - 42
14. a - 8
15. b - 3
16. Jaime Alguesuari
17. Giancarlo Fisichella
18. c - 2 hours 41 minutes
19. Australian GP
20. Blue & Yellow

2010s

1. Mark Webber
2. d - 34
3. b - 12th
4. Concussion in testing
5. a - 1st lap
6. b - 5 days
7. Sebastian Vettel
8. c - 4
9. Switched the boards
10. b - 15 points
11. Bruno Senna
12. c - 6
13. d - 52
14. 3
15. Heikki Kovalainen
16. a - Indian GP
17. Team orders
18. Lewis Hamilton & Nico Rosberg
19. Mercedes
20. Paul Di Resta